Stop Pitching & Start Networking!

Proven, effective networking strategies (that really work!) to boost your business from The Connection Queen

Biba Pédron

ISBN: 1511819588
ISBN-13: 978-1511819589

The "real life" useful networking lessons revealed in this book can only come from power networker, Biba Pédron. For networking in the 21st century, Biba's solutions oriented networking is a winning strategy that works.

Carl E. Reid, Successful Entrepreneur
www.savvyintrapreneur.com
Author of 10 Powerful Networking Tips of Influential People

As CEO of my own executive coaching and leadership skills training company, I know the importance of making and maintaining meaningful professional connections. Effective networking is a necessary skill for entrepreneurs and business professionals who want to succeed professionally and financially. However, the fact is that many people are not aware about the importance of networking or fail to do it well. The result is failure to attract new clients, lost business opportunities, or potential damage to their brand.

Biba Pédron has written an important book about the dos and don'ts of networking that takes the reader though essential elements of effective networking including: creating networking strategies; targeting the appropriate market and ideal client; knowing what to say to create a lasting impression and build your brand; and even how to construct a business card that gets your business noticed. If you want to succeed and connect with the right people to help your business grow, you need to read Stop Pitching & Start Networking! and save yourself time, money and effort. It's the go-to resource to take your business to the next level.

Jacinth Tracey, PhD - Founder and CEO at Wired2Succeed
Best Selling Author of Dump Your Fear and Claim Your Power! and Shut the BUT up! How to Stop Making the 50 Life-Stealing Excuses that Keep You Stuck, Broke and Powerless

As I read Biba's book, I realized she was teaching me the entire foundation of networking. Succinctly written, she includes every component to have a thriving business, leveraging networking to boost income. Each step is simple, easy to understand, and apply. As a master of achievement, I especially liked that Biba included self-assessment and accountability, careful documentations, and gathering statistics which builds the muscle of confidence in business. While I have heard many of these things at one time or another, Biba's careful organization of this book allowed me to easily imagine myself doing everything she advises. I'll use it as my go-to reference to review before I attend my next networking event.

Leslie Flowers
www.leslie-flowers.com
Best Selling Author of Champion. 21st Century Women: Guardians of Wealth & Legacy

If you want to make more money in your business 'Stop Pitching & Start Networking" is for you. From the basics of getting started to the step-by-step details, it's all covered in this comprehensive guide by The Connection Queen herself. Even though I thought I was pretty good at networking, I learned Biba's advanced strategies of connecting and her insider secrets to follow up. I'm implementing her systems into my business immediately! This book is a keeper that I will keep referring back to over and over again. I highly recommend reading this book, it's filled with amazing golden nuggets and strategies that will propel your business to the top!

Michelle Brubaker
www.MichelleBrubaker.com
Author of The Amazing Power of Testimonials and How to Receive Them

I highly recommend this to everyone. If you are new to networking or if you already are networking, this book is still a wonderful asset. You have nothing to lose and so much to gain. It is a MUST READ!

Corine La Font - Self Publishing, Online Marketing & Virtual Events Specialist and Consultant
www.helpdeskja.com

Congratulations Biba for truly setting a dynamic example for why you are called "The Connection Queen". Your book "Stop Pitching and Start Networking" is a tool all business owners should have in their hands. In my 20+ years of working with individuals striving for success, I am amazed how many people are missing simple opportunities to connect with the right people. It is so powerful to have a goal when networking and follow up is the difference between captured connections and missed possibilities.

Grab a highlighter pen and make note of the areas you need to work on when you are networking next. My successful business is a direct result of effective networking skills!

Jacqueline Nichols, Owner and Flirt Expert of Awaken Your Future

www.awakenyourfuture.com

For anyone struggling with networking, Biba Pédron, The Connection Queen, has written a book exclusively for you. Stop Pitching and Start Networking provides a step-by-step, pragmatic approach that gives the reader immediate results. This book teaches powerful techniques that guarantee networking success. If you have been dreaming of starting a business, or if your current business needs a boost to reach the next level, this book tells you exactly how to use networking to reach your goals.

Tara Pogoda, The Leadership Expert

www.FifthElementRanch.com
www.CouragePowerSuccess.com

Biba has done it again! In her new book, Stop Pitching & Start Networking, Biba Pédron gives everyone, from the novice entrepreneur to the most seasoned business person, the road map for networking success.

Step by step you are guided through the process so that you too can use networking as a marketing tool to grow your business to incredible heights.

Anne Kleinman - founder of Ad Infinitum

www.adinfinitumcorporate.com

v

Networking is one of those must-have business skills – and it's one that everybody thinks they know how to correctly utilize. Biba has written a "back to the basics" primer on networking that reminds experienced entrepreneurs of skills they may have lost and gives new business owners all the tools they need not only to network effectively but also how to network with confidence! I'll be giving copies of Biba's books to several of my associates who are Nervous Networkers because I know this is the book that will make the difference in their confidence and long-term business success.

Kim Eldredge, Best-selling author, President of New Frontier Books
www.NewFrontierBooks.com
Story Pathfinder * Intuitive Ghostwriter * New Frontier Publisher

*With love to the wind beneath my wings, my parents,
Liliane and Michel, who always support me.*

Contents

Networking 101:
Back To Basics

My love affair with networking started in 2002 when I came to New York to start a new business and discovered this new world. I didn't know anything about networking; not even what the word meant. I was surprised that everywhere I went, each time I met someone, they tended to give me their business card in the first few seconds. I was wondering why I should need their business cards when I hardly knew them?

Then I discovered networking events. I still remember the very first networking event that I attended in New York. I discovered the event on the Internet. I arrived in a crowded bar, very noisy, took my namctag, and looked around. I was so intimidated that I left in less than two minutes and said, *"Ok, this networking thing is definitely not for me."*

Looking back, this is quite funny when you consider that I run a business that organizes and facilitates networking events for years to help other entrepreneurs grow their businesses using networking effectively.

My clients even call me **"The Connection Queen".**

After the first networking event I attended, I decided to explore more and understand why it was so popular and what I could get out of it for my business.

Everyone needs to network

Entrepreneurs, small business owners, job seekers! But after spending the last few years organizing business networking events, I still don't have the answer to why some people attend those events.

But does everyone maximize the benefits of networking?

The purpose of networking is to build relationships so you will get leads from someone you know, or from someone who knows someone you know. When you attend a networking event, the purpose is to meet business people from various industries to get exposure.

What networking isn't

Networking is not a numbers game; you need to focus on quality and not on quantity.

The only goal for most people who attend networking events seems to be to collect business cards. They have the feeling of a great event if they come back home with 30 or more business cards.

Some people think that they had a successful event when they have collected 30, 40 or more business cards, but they are missing the real point. How many of these 30 or 40 people will you be able to follow-up? How many of these 30 or 40 will follow-up with you? What is the purpose of collecting a huge number of business cards that will end up in a shoe-box on one of your shelves?

Networking is not a place to sell. You have to be prepared to give your elevator pitch to introduce yourself, not give a sales pitch. If you attend an event expecting to find a client to close a sale right away, chances are you will be very disappointed. Furthermore, the other attendees might not appreciate your attitude.

What networking is

Networking is more than just shaking hands and collecting business cards. It is about building relationships and being committed to help other business professionals. It is about the quality of your contacts and not the amount of your contacts.

What is your goal when you attend a networking event? Are you trying to get new contacts to buy your product or service, or do you give the opportunity for people to get to know you, as the first step of your networking system?

People are always surprised in my trainings when I say that I never try to sell anything during an event. One of my secrets is that my business card mentions, "The Connection Queen", which usually gets me lots of comments and questions: "How do you speak with strangers?" or "How do you introduce yourself without being pitchy?" or "How to you leave people if you are not interested in what they are doing?" and so on.

So why do you network?

Try to think of your strategy for a moment. Test different approaches; stop selling and start implementing a follow-up system. You will get many more results and will attract your ideal clients, and only your ideal clients--the ones who really appreciate your services. Clients who like and trust you, clients who respect your knowledge and experience, and, very importantly, clients who will work with you in the long term and will refer you to people like them. This means more ideal clients.

I attend networking events to build a long-term relationship with people, not to collect business cards or to sell anything. My only purpose is to listen to people and see how I can give them a contact, a resource, or some advice. It shows them my expertise without selling anything, but offering them my free ebook, "15 Ways to Instantly Skyrocket Your Networking Results", (you can find it at www.bibapedron.com/free-gift) to find the answers to all of their questions.

Offering them my free ebook and video series is a way to get them to sign-up for my weekly newsletter and have a chance to get to know me, trust me, and later, to buy my product or service, but only when they are ready.

A fortune in follow up

How many of you follow up with everybody after each event? How many people who you met followed up with you?

I recently attended a business expo, and, of course I met a number of people. I didn't take everybody's business cards, only the ones I had an interest in. I also spoke with the owners of two different booths because they had a product I was interested in purchasing. I asked all of my questions, explained why I needed the product, gave them my card, and asked them to contact me to close the sale after the expo. This was a very easy sell for them, but guess what? None of them followed up with me or even returned my e-mails. Well, they both lost a sale, because I didn't find them to be very professional.

I guess that if they didn't follow-up with me, chances are that they didn't follow-up with other people either. So what was the purpose of having a table at this expo?

When I train people on networking, either one-on-one or in a group and ask those two questions, I usually have the same answer.

"Oh yes I follow-up, I send an email the next day." My next question is, "What do you do after this email?" and the usual answer is, "Well, nothing, because I don't know what to do next."

So what is the purpose of spending two to three hours at a networking event and pay $20 to $50 each time, if it is just to go and say hello to some people who you will never contact again? Repeat the process two to three times a week, and this is a big waste of time AND money.

Networking Is about Consistency

The best is to belong to two or three groups, attend their events regularly, get to know the other members, and in exchange, they will get to know you and trust you. When you see the same people over and over, you develop a strong relationship with them. The benefit of building relationships with a committed group of people will result in new leads for your business.

Networking is about patience

The benefit will not appear overnight, and this is why you need to follow up with your contacts. Networking is like dating, one meeting is not enough to know someone. It will probably take some time, some meetings, some lunches or some drinks before you really start doing business together.

PART I
Beginning Steps
To Networking

CHAPTER 1
Create Your Networking Action Plan

Time goes so fast! We usually don't have enough time to do everything we would like. I am sure you probably write your to-do list in the morning, and when the evening comes, you still have a lot to accomplish from it. You got distracted during the day, something happened, and you ran late.

Well, it is the same thing with New Year's resolutions. We have a lot in mind in December, but by the end of January, the priorities we set up are gone for X, Y, Z reasons.

What were your networking strategies for this year? Did you check the results at the end of last year?

- How many networking events did you attend?
- How many groups did you join?
- How many new contacts did you make, per month, and during the year?
- How many of these new contacts became paying clients?
- How many of your current clients reorder from you?
- How many referrals did you get from your clients or

contacts?
- What is your conversion rate?

Did you ever ask yourself any of those questions?

If you didn't ask yourself those questions at the end of the year, it is urgent to do this right now. The economy has been pretty bad lately, so if you don't change your strategies to get better results, you can expect this year to be a very bad year for you.

So take a moment, and write down everything you did to promote your business: networking, marketing, communication, etc.

Whatever you did, did you do it only once or multiple times? For example, if you did a postcard mailing, did you send only one card per contact or a series of cards? The same thing goes if you put an ad in a newspaper or on the Internet. After how many times did you notice a result?

Statistics show that we need to see or hear a message at least 10 to 16 times *before we even notice it,* so make sure you don't give up after only a couple of attempts.

How did you follow-up with people? Do you have a follow-up system in place to make sure that you always know what to do when you meet somebody new, either at a networking event or any place else?

Did you send them an email and eventually call a few days later, and stop there, like most people do and claim that networking is not working?

Did you create a free report, or a free CD to send to people to let them know more about your business?

Did you update your website, and mention all of your new services or products, and inform everybody that you created new services during the year?

Did you organize teleclasses or webinars to reach more people in one time instead of meeting individual people one at a time?

Did you create partnerships with other entrepreneurs to offer more services to your clients?

What worked best for you in the last year?

What did you do to change the way you were doing business before? What didn't work, and did you analyze why?

With all of your answers, create an action plan to do more of what worked last year and see how you could even double this result this year.

To make sure these strategies will be in place for the entire year, **schedule a meeting with yourself every week,** to test, track, and analyze everything you do. So you will not spend months wondering how you should grow your business.

This meeting with yourself should be your most important meeting of the week.

You are your most important client! All the time you spend working on your business instead of working in your business will generate more and more clients for you – and obviously more money for your business.

Create an Excel document with your networking goals for the year and report all of your results and update per date, so you will not forget and put every positive result in red, so each time you look at it, you will know exactly where you are, and where you are going.

CHAPTER 2
Network With Your
Target Market

One of the biggest misconceptions that solo-entrepreneurs have is that they **expect to sell to everyone and anyone.**

This misconception creates a huge problem across the board. At networking events when I ask, **"Who is your target market?"** to understand better how I can help someone, a lot of people answer, "Everybody, really. My products or services can serve everybody."

Each time I hear this answer I tend to lose interest in the conversation, because I know that those people have no clue on how to market their business. You are setting yourself up for major disappointment if you expect to make money working this way. Attending networking events, talking to everyone about your services no matter what their needs, is not going to provide you with results. And frankly, I'm tired of hearing this nonsense.

The very first step when you start a business is to determine your niche and target market. You build your list based on people and businesses that have a use for your products. You are not going to convince anyone who has no need for your product to become a client.

Unfortunately, too many people continue to get frustrated, not knowing why their business is failing; because heck, they have a huge list, they include everyone, and there must be someone out there who wants their product! If you try to sell to anyone and everyone you're just letting a balloon drift into the air expecting that someone will catch it, but up it goes and eventually disappears into the sky. When it lands it's deflated and out of air. You're suffocating your business!

Know your target market. Create your marketing tools, websites, business cards, flyers, postcards, articles, blogs, newsletters, etc., directed at your target market's interests. When your contacts see your materials, they will know you took the time to make something for them, something that will solve their problems; and you will become the person they look to for guidance when they need it most.

You become The Solution.

Recently someone contacted me via a LinkedIn message with the title "We need your help!" After exchanging a couple of introductory emails, he explained his company's problems. When I asked him what motivated him to pick up the phone when I rang his answer was, "I saw some of your posts on LinkedIn, read some of your articles online, checked your blog, and you definitely seem to know what you are talking about regarding a business through networking, and that is exactly what we need right now."

Lots of my materials, articles, tweets, or blog posts, are about networking. I explain what issues my target market has and how my knowledge and expertise can solve them. When people see the consistency of my marketing tools they come looking for me; I don't have to go looking for clients. Create your marketing materials, your solutions, your pitch at your prospective client base, and they will recognize themselves and decide to work with you and nobody else.

Building your business around your target market will help you attract a lot more clients in record time.

CHAPTER 3
The Elevator Pitch: 60 Seconds to Networking Success

As a small business owner, you have various marketing options to promote your business: advertising, telemarketing, direct mail. But my favorite is definitely networking. First, it is the most low-cost marketing tool, and second, it is a way to build long-term relationships with people. If advertising can give you a great result in one shot, networking will bring you more in the long run.

Since 2003, when I started my business in the United States, I organized many business networking events, which were a great opportunity for me to meet a tremendous amount of people, make deals, get clients, make friends and learn from others entrepreneurs.

During those events, I also noticed that a significant number of people had great products or services, but just didn't know how to present them. And as a result were not able to attract the clients they were looking for.

One of the keys to networking is to be able to introduce yourself and your business in 30 to 60 seconds or less, in one or two sentences, in a very concise way. In other words, you need to have a very efficient elevator pitch. You should be ready to deliver your elevator pitch in the blink of an eye at a moment's notice.

But what *is* an elevator pitch?

An elevator pitch is a short presentation that introduces you and your business's mission and makes you memorable. It focuses on the benefits you provide, and can be delivered in 30-60 seconds or less, even in an elevator, hence the name. If you are passionate, excited and eager to create and manage your own business, then you should be able to describe, in one or two brief and concise sentences, exactly what you do, why your offering is the best in the marketplace, and in effect, why the person should buy from you.

The best way to develop your elevator pitch is to summarize or list the most enticing, exciting and valuable benefits that your customers will get when they use your products and services. How can your products and services solve problems or meet needs?

An effective elevator pitch makes a lasting impression, demonstrates your professionalism and allows you to position yourself with your target customers. Remember that your client's main concern is: "What benefits will I receive when I buy your product or service?" So when you prepare your elevator pitch always make sure that your audience answers this question: "What's in it for me?"

People are always more interested in how you can help them than in what you do or how they can help you.

Consider these points when you develop your elevator pitch:

1. **Write down the "deliverables."** The products, services and features that you provide. Then, analyze your offering and put yourself in your customers' shoes. What good things will they get or what good things will happen to them when they make a purchase?
2. **Be specific.** Use numbers and statistics when you can. For example: double your revenue in less than 12 months; achieve a 30% increase over last year; lose 20 pounds in 10 weeks; triple your number of subscribers in 5 days or less, etc. People are driven by numbers because they add a sense

of credibility to a claim. Numbers also generate curiosity and anxiety, another useful tool that motivates people to make a purchase.

3. **Never reveal your entire story in your elevator pitch.** Highlight the main benefits your products and/or services provided, which will encourage people to ask questions and start the conversation.

4. **Create a tagline that grabs your listener's attention!** And forces him or her to stop what he or she is doing and listen to you. The most effective openers leave the audience seeking additional information. Compare your elevator pitch to the cover of your favorite magazine. Most likely, you'll find the titles of the key stories in that issue. If the titles don't grab your attention and raise your curiosity quickly, then you probably won't buy that issue.

5. **Practice your elevator pitch.** You'll want to practice it to the point where you can recite the language with perfect ease, great confidence and clarity and total poise immediately. It is extremely important that you feel totally comfortable whenever you deliver your elevator pitch. Learn it; practice it; master it; but never read it. Your delivery must be very smooth and totally fluid.

Continually practice your elevator pitch in front of the mirror and before your friends until your Pitch becomes a part of you.

Do you have a better idea? Are you ready to write your elevator pitch? Try this the next time you describe what you do. Choose your words. Hook your listener. Make them ask questions. Make them want to meet with you and buy your products and services.

CHAPTER 4
First Contact

Entrepreneurs with businesses in early start-up differ on what they believe to be the most important element, although many professionals will argue that creating a solid business plan should definitely be the first step. A well-crafted business plan lays out all the details and strategies, includes projections for revenue and spending, and will be reviewed in detail by bankers and venture capitalists. But in fact, the most important document that should be created even before the business plan is the **"elevator pitch."**

The fact is most people won't read a business plan unless they have been motivated to do so beforehand. **The elevator pitch is that motivating factor.** It's the hook that gets them into the room. It's the catchy jingle that gets people to pay attention to the ad. It's the best part of the business plan, without the boring details. The elevator pitch is the place for the excitement, not the place to include all the technology, buzzwords and explanations.

An elevator pitch should be able to be condensed into a single-page presentation, short enough to be memorized, or read easily within a few minutes – that's how it got its name: it's a pitch that's short enough to be presented during the course of an elevator ride. The elevator pitch condenses your business concept into something that can be presented in about a minute or two—essentially, the parts that matter, the very "essence" of the business.

The elevator pitch skips the hard-core financials, and gets straight to the heart of what it is about the business that really gets you excited. That's what this pitch is about—you don't need the proof of concept here yet, that comes in the full-length business plan.

The elevator pitch is the commercial that gets people interested.

The elevator pitch should be inspirational and creative, hitting the high points of your business concept, and should accomplish the following:

- Hit the high points of what it is you hope to do
- Summarize the problem/solution aspect of your concept
- Describe the business model—how is it going to make money?
- Create excitement on the part of the reader/listener
- Describe the profit potential without having to bring out charts and graphs
- Tell why you/your company are well positioned to accomplish your goal
- End with a call to action

The first couple sentences are the most critical, and should present your core concept. If you can't tell what it is you want to do in two sentences or less, then you need to simplify your concept. There will be plenty of time to get into all the details later, once you've captured your audience's interest.

CHAPTER 5
How to Brand Yourself & Your Business in 30 Seconds

Did you ever meet a person at a networking event and had to think before you answered "What do you do?"

Did you ever notice how some people stumble when they are asked the defining question? Or some people just go on and on and after 5 minutes of non-stop explanation, you still don't really understand the purpose of their business? I guess at some point you were in one of these positions, if not both! How can you introduce yourself and your business in just 30 seconds, making sure you deliver both your brand and benefits of your services?

Here are the top 3 key elements to brand yourself in 30 Seconds:

1. Perfect your Elevator Pitch

You want to be ready at any time so you need to prepare your answer in advance and rehearse it. The next time somebody asks you "What do you do?" you shouldn't have to think of an answer.

Start your elevator pitch by mentioning very clearly who is your target market and what their needs are: their problem. In just one or two sentences explain the benefit of your services and how you bring the solution to this target market.

Please don't say "Oh my service is for everybody!" because it isn't. If you don't have a target market with a common problem you can solve, you can't grow your business. And remember, you won't be able to grow your business if you don't know who your target market is. Take a few seconds to explain what makes you different from your competitors. What is your unique selling position? Don't try to be technical or use jargon from your industry because this generally causes people's attention to wander. Use the formula KISS (Keep It Short and Simple).

Be cautious not to tell your whole story. Instead, hook your audience; intrigue them so they'll ask you questions about you and your business. Think as if you were introducing yourself on Twitter, but instead of 140 characters, you have a few sentences to work with.

Always finish your elevator pitch with a call to action. Tell people what to do next: go to your website, sign-up for your newsletter for free report, call you for a free consultation, etc…

Practice, practice, practice! Test your elevator pitch on friends or colleagues and get their feedback. Rehearse it until you sound natural and not like reading. Say it in front of the mirror. Practice and perfect your elevator pitch to get more contacts and clients!

2. Make your Business Card Stand Out

The second step after you deliver your elevator pitch to somebody at a networking event, or after any contact, is to give your business card. If you have an effective elevator pitch but then give a crappy business card, you just lost a new potential contact. You need to have a professional image. Remember to use the back of the card to highlight the benefits of using your product or services.

Remember: your business card is an important marketing tool.

Use it to attract potential clients and not only to provide your contact information. Use it to pass on your business message and new clients will respond.

After you give your business card a makeover to make sure you will start the year with the most effective marketing message, please, please, avoid printing them yourself on your printer. It doesn't cost a lot to print professional business cards. You can order a thousand for $40 or less online. You can even print your business cards by 100 or 200 and change the message on a regular basis. It doesn't cost a lot more to print on both sides, but it does make an incredible difference and has a greater impact on people.

Promote your business the right way. Don't kill your effect with a non-professional business card.

3. Have a Professional Website

Obviously you don't have time to say everything you want to in 30 seconds. Your business card can't say everything either. A professional website is your greatest tool to spread effective information about you, your business, your products or services, and the benefits of working with you.

To focus on your branding, again use the same color on all of your marketing tools, business card, flyers, post cards, website etc. Having a streamlined look will ensure that people will recognize you as soon as they see your materials. If you use different colors or logos on each material, people can feel lost and as a result they will never contact you.

Now that you attracted them to your website, make sure they don't leave without taking action. You can have a nice and flashy website, but without a direct purpose and a call to action, the extra money you spend on website is wasted. You'll need an opt-in box on each and every page of your website; you never know on which page they'll decide to sign-up. You will also need an incentive for them to sign-up. Offering a bit of valuable information for free right away is the best option. Just mentioning "sign-up for my newsletter" won't do the trick.

The other advantage of having an opt-in box is you know you are contacting your target market. Who else would sign up for your newsletter? If people are not interested in your services, they won't give you their information. It's as simple as that.

Those 3 key elements will help you to build the perfect branding while reaching your target market and building your list. They work as a package, so make sure to not miss one of these important steps to grow your business.

CHAPTER 6
Never Leave Without Your Business Cards

Because your business card is your first marketing tool, you want it to make the right impression. So I always mention: "Never leave the house without your business cards!" You can have THE best business card in the world, but if you don't have it with you, it's useless!

Since I practice what I preach, of course I always carry my business cards with me.

Order professional business cards. This helps to portray your image, which makes you stand out from the crowd. The card helps people you meet remember you and makes it easier for those people to contact you again, or to give your card (information) to other people as a referral.

That is your first marketing tool that will make a difference. People tend to keep business cards in a business card file, book or Rolodex®, or they enter the data in their electronic organizer.

Never leave home without your business cards. Wherever you go – to a networking event, to the dentist, to the movies, to a party, always bring your business cards with you. You never know where you will meet an interesting new contact, and you don't want to miss the opportunity to exchange cards. Writing your telephone number or email address on a piece of paper or a paper napkin, doesn't look very professional.

Always carry a pen to take notes on the back of the cards you receive – something you would like to remember about the person, something they said, something you have promised to send them.

Use your business card as a marketing tool to help you stand out from the crowd.

Don't put only your name and address, but add your logo. I know it may sound obvious, but many professionals don't have a logo at least on their card. Add your website address, so people can check it later to learn more about your business. Ad your tagline which explains your business in one line; if you don't have tagline or slogan, it is time to think about it.

Let's say you are a coach or a financial advisor, no doubt, you have a lot of competition. What makes you unique and special? When people see your card, they will probably say, "Oh, another one!" but if you mentioned your specialties on your card, it will make a difference immediately.

Years ago, before teaching networking, I had the problem of going out without my business cards from time to time, especially when I was using a new hand bag. So today, I have found the solution. I have about 30 handbags (I know, women, we can be obsessive with fashion sometimes) and carry 3 things in each of them:

1. A pen because you often need to take notes, well I do
2. Pills for my migraines, that can happen anytime, and
3. Business cards, then I just have to transfer my wallet from one bag to another depending on which one I use. Since I never leave the house without a handbag, I am always sure to have business cards with me and always ready to network.

Well almost, there is ONLY one place where I don't take a handbag. When I go to the pool in my building! I didn't think I would need one... until that fateful weekend!

Like every Saturday, I went to the pool to spend the afternoon. One of my neighbors introduced me to one of his friends who was visiting for few days. His friend was from Switzerland so he speaks French too. We started speaking about the weather, his vacation, and some chit chat until he asked the question, "And what do you do?"

So I explained my consulting services for Europeans who come to start their business in the US or want to invest in real estate in Miami, mentioning how I build various networks and work with people like lawyers, bankers, CPAs, real estate agents, mortgage brokers, and other consultants.

He was suddenly very interested since he was considering buying a condo in Miami by the end of the year. So I happened to do a consultation while we were swimming, which was a first for me, but you never know when and where you will meet your next client. After two hours in the pool he had to leave, so of course he asked for my contact information and phone number. Guess what! I didn't have my business cards with me and no pen and nothing to put my information down. That is when I realized that from now on, **I will have my business cards with me EVERYWHERE, ALL THE TIME,** *even at the pool.* Well lucky for me he was still there on Sunday, so I gave him my card the next day, still at the pool, but what would have happened if I didn't get the chance to see him again? I would lose a potential client!

Three days later, back in Switzerland he called me to start the process to help him to select and buy a condo.

Lesson learned!

NEVER EVER leave the house without your business cards.

You definitely never know when and where you will meet your next client. Always be ready to do business any time, in any circumstance. If others don't have their business cards with them, you will be sure that you can give your contact information. People who need your product or service will be able to reach you, and more importantly you will never lose the opportunity to make a sale.

CHAPTER 7
How to Make Sure Your Business Card Gets Noticed

Having organized and attended networking events for years, I'm still always surprised and amazed to see how many small business owners don't have business cards or don't have professional business cards. Having a professional business card helps portray your business image and make you stand out from the crowd. When you meet somebody you have less than 10 seconds to make the right first impression and your business card can help make sure people will remember you.

Your business card is your first marketing tool. Are you using it in the most effective way?

Many small business owners spend hours and hours trying to find the best way of marketing their businesses. But when it comes to their business cards they don't follow the same rules. Most people just include their basic contact information and don't realize how this little piece of paper can say a lot about their businesses.

When you place an ad in a newspaper or magazine, don't you try to write the most effective text to attract clients so people buy your products or services? So why not pay the same attention when designing your business card.

Your business card is your first marketing tool. Every time you give it to somebody is a chance to communicate something about your business. Your business card is often the tool which will help people decide whether they want to work with you; it's an extension of your business. When you meet somebody for the first time they'll judge you on your appearance, your clothes, the way you act, the way you speak, AND YOUR BUSINESS CARD If the whole package looks professional they'll be willing to continue the conversation with you. If it doesn't look professional they won't waste their time and will find somebody else to work with.

We used to say we shouldn't judge a book by its cover, but unfortunately people do. So put all the chances on your side.

Here are the 10 indispensable keys which need to appear on your business card:

On the front of your card:

1. Your name – this may sound obvious, but make sure it's easy to find. People need to see your name as soon as they receive your card so they'll be able to associate your face with the name on the card. This will help them to remember you.

2. Your title – if you work for a corporation, your title is always mentioned on the card. If you're a small business owner, it's important to mention if you're the founder, the CEO, the president, etc. Again, make it easy for people to remember you and what you do.

3. The name of your company – even if you're a one person operation, it's important to have a business name. Only using your name and not your company name gives the image of a part-time activity and not a serious business. It's the same as when you introduce yourself and say, "I'm a consultant" vs "I own a consulting company." Even if your consulting company is only you, this will have more impact. People won't pursue you in the same way if they can't take you seriously.

4. Your email address –don't use an email with yahoo, AOL, Gmail, or Hotmail, account. Have a professional email with yourname@yourdomainname.com. It doesn't cost a lot to buy a domain name so please invest the $10 to $15 to buy a domain and use it on your business card.

You can have a free email address you use to subscribe to newsletters or for your personal correspondence, but is shows a lack of professionalism on your business card. Plus it's much easier for people to remember your name and your company name than a strange email with your nickname!

5. Your phone number – use the best number for people to reach you. Personally I think too many phone numbers are confusing and take up too much space. I recommend you use your main number, even if it is your cell phone, because it's the most convenient way to reach you.

6. Your website – having a website will help people to learn more about your business. Your business card can't say everything, so give them the opportunity to get the information they're looking for. Use your business card to bring traffic to your website. You can also mention your social media links.

7. Your logo – it's as important to have a logo as it is to have a business name. Again, it gives you a professional image. Using a white card with no logo, and just your name, phone number and email won't help people remember you. Some people use clipart on their business card and think it looks like a logo. In people's minds this is definitely not the same thing! If you aren't ready to invest in yourself how do you expect people to invest in you?

8. Your tagline – a tagline ensures people associate your company name with your product or service. A tagline is a short sentence describing your business mission and what makes you unique. It's is usually the only thing people remember after you've met. It's important to choose your words carefully when creating your tagline so you hook your audience and are memorable.

Just because you're a small business owner doesn't mean you can't use the same strategies as the big companies. Make sure you use all the marketing tools available to promote your business. This is called 'branding'. Using an effective logo & tagline are one of the most effective ways to successfully brand your business.

Take a look at most of the business cards you've collected and you'll notice few of them have taglines. Stand out from the crowd and make sure to have the key elements on your card and that they are memorable.

On the back of your card:

When I work with a client and help him or her redesign their business card, I always encourage them to use the back of the card. Remember what I said earlier, "When you place an ad in a newspaper or magazine, don't you try to write the most effective text to attract clients so people buy your products or services?"

Why are you wasting the precious space on the back of your card?

Remember your business card is a marketing tool. Use it to attract potential clients and not just to provide your contact information. Use it to pass on your business message. Few people use the back of their cards so here's an opportunity for you to be different.

9. Describe the benefits of your product or service or the benefits of working with you. Use bullet points to emphasize the purpose of your products and services. Show how you can solve their problem. Encourage people to ask you questions about your business so they want to learn more and visit your website later.

10. Tell people what to do next. Don't assume people will contact you for more information: tell them what to do. Do you want them to go to your website, sign-up for your newsletter, call you, or buy your product? Tell them clearly what the next step is. And offer an incentive to make sure they'll take action.

Let's say you're a coach or a financial advisor; no doubt, you have a lot of competition. What makes you unique and special? When people see your card, they will probably say, "Oh, another one!" But if you mentioned your specialties on your card it makes an immediate difference.

What's on your Business Card?

Take a look at your card now:
- Does it include the key elements to give a professional image to your business?
- Does your card stand out from the crowd?
- Does your card give you the results you are expecting?
- Does your card say what you want it to say?
- Does your card's design work with your company image and the rest of your marketing materials?

If you have one design for your business card, a second design for your website and a third for your brochure, how do you expect people to take you seriously? Your business card is an extension of your company just like your logo, letter head, brochures, flyers, website, and any marketing tools. They must all have the same message and design.

Order professional business cards. Avoid cards you print yourself. It doesn't cost a lot to print professional business cards; you can order a thousand for $40 to $60 online and it doesn't cost much more to print on both sides of your card. But it makes an incredible difference and has a greater impact on people.

Use the same logo and colors as your website, brochure, or flyer. Having consistency on your marketing materials will help people to recognize you wherever they see you. The more they see you or your logo, the more they'll remember you and the more they'll keep in touch with you. Try to always be at the forefront of their minds.

And never leave home without your business cards! Wherever you go, to a networking event, to the dentist, to the movies, to a party, always bring your business cards with you. You never know where you'll meet an interesting new contact and you don't want to miss the opportunity to exchange cards. Writing your telephone number or email address on a piece of paper or napkin doesn't look very professional.

CHAPTER 8
The Art Of Giving
Business Cards

Giving business cards is an art, not only because they are needed to be considered successful or because, in fact, they represent your corporate or professional identity, but also as an opportunity to impact your existing or prospective customers, and stay in touch with them, helping you to deal confidently.

The scope of business etiquette includes considerations that many professional ignore, or simply do not pay enough attention in the belief that a business card is just a small paper rectangle with a name and phone numbers to introduce yourself.

Color business cards demonstrate that there is something else beyond a simple paper cut; otherwise, they simply would not exist. Certainly, all over the world business cards are used to provide information about a company and/or the employee or professional who holds it, as well as contact information and other details such as business acquaintances or personal details.

Some of them include expressly empty spaces to write certain details such as an appointment date, some others are as simple as blank cards that come in handy when the holder has to leave a customer further details. However, those in color are undoubtedly part of a practical business strategy following refined business etiquette.

In business, time is gold and every minute is important because more often an individual only has a few minutes to impress a prospective client, before someone else does it first.

Gentle manners can conquer, but accompanied with poor business cards, it is more likely the client will forget about you as soon as you leave. Unprofessional business cards will not impress but will leave your prospective client with negative thoughts about your company.

On the other hand, color business cards are attractive and catch the eye of even the most skeptical business contact. There is nothing more accurate that "a picture is worth a thousand words" when it comes to describing the first impression left on a person who receives a business card especially crafted to achieve a predefined business goal.

All business cards should be printed on very high quality paper, designed by professionals, and never using public domain graphics, clip art, or other elements that makes them look cheap.

Make sure to include all personal information for your business acquaintances, and always carry enough of them with you, particularly when you are planning to attend a business meeting or social event.

The art of business cards is not only in giving them away, but also in exchanging and receiving. Every time you attend an event where other professionals participate, try to exchange business cards with them, particularly color business cards to better impress, and when you receive a business card, study its design and content because you can learn from them.

Finally, always keep in mind that business cards are the branding tool of your company, not just a piece of paper to stay in touch with someone else.

PART II
How To Network

CHAPTER 9
Turn Your Shyness Into A Networking Resource

Networking is an integral part of today's business and personal world. Everyone agrees that networking is a must to grow a business. Yet many people have challenges on how to effectively use and integrate connections in their business.

The most important aspect of networking is your first impression.

Are you prepared to walk the room? Do you know when and how to start and end conversations? Do you have the right follow-up plan to solidify your connections?

Shyness is a problem with many attendees. The fear of your own shyness can be debilitating. You can overcome your shyness by following a clear step-by-step plan.

I have always been a shy person. When I started attending events in New York, I had two major challenges. First, I was shy; I didn't know how to approach people; and second, my English was not fluent; even when people started speaking with me I had trouble understanding what they said. It was not an ideal way to communicate effectively.

At first I used to stay in a corner, waiting for people to come to me. But after a while, I noticed other shy people who were alone. I decided to speak with them because they seemed to be more like me. Our combined shyness turned out to be an asset to connect with each other and build confidence, instead of using our shyness as an excuse or a hindrance.

Turn your negatives into positives.

I usually started a conversation with another shy person like this: "Hi, is it your first time in this group?" or "Hi, I like your dress or jacket"; anything that could help me start the conversation. Then if the person was open to speak, I would follow the conversation and at some point we would speak about our businesses. I don't jump into business right away. My strategy is to establish a connection about something other than business and tie it into our businesses later in the conversation.

After finally getting my feet wet with one person, I fell into another shyness trap: sticking to the same person for too long. Since it was so difficult for me to start speaking with one person, I would tend to never leave his or her side for fear of having to deal with my shyness once again. This defeats the purpose of a networking event, which is to promote your service or product by connecting with as many people possible in a short period of time.

You should spend no more than five to ten minutes per conservation by following my step-by-step networking playbook. Introduce yourself and let them introduce themselves. Talk about your business and leave an opportunity to follow-up with them later, and then close the conversation and let them go to meet other people.

If you're shy, don't try to break up a group of people. You will be setting yourself up for failure, which will feed your shyness bug. Remember to look for other people who are alone and approach them. Start with a casual conversation: ask them if it is their first time in this group, if they know anybody in the room, if they already have clients or referrals from this group, and then ask about their business.

Networking is about listening. It is much more important to listen to what people have to say and try to help them and solve their problem, than to tell your story. Being shy is an advantage because you take more care to observe the room before jumping in and because you are a good listener. People love to talk and their favorite things to talk about are things they are proud of. What makes you an ideal contact is the fact you listen to ideas and descriptions of businesses that make sense, and you'll remember them the next time you meet.

Extroverts can have a tendency to jump from person to person while giving their own few minutes of speech and moving on. Instead of caring about what the other person has to say, they deliver their own spiel and don't even give the potential contact the time to deliver his or her elevator speech. This person will be remembered as pushy, uncaring, and flakey; or they won't be remembered at all! Not the best approach.

Use your shyness as challenge to connect meaningfully with more people, to make a better impression and to become a good listener. After all, networking *is all about them* and not about you.

Follow-up effectively, and you'll have plenty of opportunities later to introduce your business. You'll be remembered as a go-to person and a listener. And we all know that listeners are great problem solvers!

CHAPTER 10
How Well Do You Know Them?

It's often said that it's not who you know that matters, it's who knows you. Well I would like to extend this statement by saying that it's not only who you know and who knows you, but **how well do you know them and they you?**

In business, networking is the ultimate form of promotion. It can help you to obtain new clients, a new job, or even help you to move up the corporate ladder. It is the process of building relationships. Any time that you attend a meeting, networking event, trade show, or a social function, you are networking whether you realize it or not. It is the relationship that you have with people, a prospect or a client that makes the difference between success and failure.

Often we fail to realize the reasons that we have for doing business with an individual or a company. In the case of products that we regularly buy, what helps us to make the buying decision? There are those that will buy a specific brand of product because they trust that brand to be of a high quality or durability. There are others that will make a buying decision based on price, although this is less frequently the case.

Often we do business because we simply feel good about it.

In fact, most purchases or decisions to do business are based on two things: trust and comfort. Trust is a very intangible emotion or feeling. How do you measure it? How do you develop it?

Trust is measured by the feelings that are generated by a process of letting someone get to know more about you than just product, features and price. I know a gentleman who provides a seminar on selling to C-level executives. He says that to sell to the C-level executive you have to be more than a salesperson selling a product or service. To sell to the executive level, you have to be more of an advisor. You have to find needs other than the ones that you can fulfill and help them to fulfill these needs. In doing this, you become a "trusted advisor". They feel "comfortable" that you have their interests in mind more than just making a quick sale and a commission.

In our daily process of seeking prospective clients, do we often just look for a person to pitch, or do we spend a bit more time getting to know them before we try to sell?

When we take the time to know a person' desires, dreams, and needs, and make an honest effort to help them realize that these things are important to us, we are really on the fast track to doing business with them. We are building the trust, confidence, comfort level, and most importantly the relationship that is needed not only to make the sale, but also to create in them a resource for endless referrals.

As we go into the community meeting people who are prospective clients, we should keep the following in mind: The customer is a person just like me. The customer has needs other than the one that I can fulfill. Until I understand what the ultimate goal or dream of the prospect is, I cannot fulfill it with my product or service.

Selling and networking are about relationships. You sell in everything that you do whether you realize it or not. The time is now for more effective selling.

Change the way you think about the prospect and the prospect will change the way that they think about you.

CHAPTER 11
Why People Give Up Before Seeing Results

Are you one of those who have nightmares about attending networking events? Do you dread meeting contacts because you have had bad results? You are not alone.

The number one problem is a perception issue:

Most people who attend networking events expect results immediately.

They attend networking events with the only purpose of making a sale right away. When a sale doesn't happen and they come home empty handed (save the hundreds of business cards in their pockets) they are disappointed.

Networking is about consistency; results don't happen overnight. You need to build relationships before your contacts even consider working with you or sending you referrals. They won't buy from you after a five to ten minute conversation.

One of the biggest mistakes in networking is a poor follow-up system. If you contact someone a couple of times, don't get the results you expect and then give up you are making a mistake. And this is a mistake that will reinforce your hatred of networking.

In marketing we say that repetition in key. Statistics show that people need to see or hear the same message at least 10 to 16 times to even notice it.

Do you follow-up at least 10 to 16 times with your contacts?

In networking consistency is key and the only way to be consistent is to have at least a 10 to 16 contact steps in your follow-up system.

In order to turn most of your contacts into paying clients, you need to have a follow-up system to keep in touch with them on a regular basis. They need to get to know you, learn more about you and your business to consider your business worthy of their time. It is not their job you get to know you, but your responsibility to give them information about you and your business on a regular basis. You do this by sending emails, mailing postcards, fliers, brochures, calling, using blogs, videos, and any other media that you can use to give them information.

What information to include is tricky. Don't give them information about you, but information about what you can do for them. You probably heard it before: "what's in it for me?" If by giving them valuable information about your services, you give them a solution to solve their problem, you win their business. When they need services they will come to you and nobody else.

Don't become frustrated! Don't stop networking with people after only 2 or 3 contacts, don't give up. Keep following-up and you will see results and will see more and more of your contacts turned clients. All you need to do is maintain consistency even when they become clients. Don't forget about them just because they bought once, keep following-up and they will become repeat clients.

If you don't have a system in your business, you don't have a business.

Give your contacts a hint of your products or services. In the long run, you will find that they will give back to you by buying from you and/or sending you referrals.

Contact more than just a few times and automate your contact process. Keep doing it and you will be surprised how people will come back to you.

CHAPTER 12
How Effective Is Your
Follow-up System?

As a solo-entrepreneur or small business owner, you probably attend lots of networking events, even if you hate networking – because you know or heard that it is the way to grow your business. The more people you speak with and introduce your products or services, more sales you will make. Well, it doesn't exactly work like this.

Attending networking events is only the first step of the process of networking. It is important to attend events not to give your sale pitch to everybody you meet but to get exposure, to meet people, so you get to know them while they get to know you. You learn more about them and try to help them, so right on the spot you can show a sample of your expertise giving them some advice, instead of trying to sell them anything.

Doing so, you attend various events a week and collect numbers of business cards. Now what do you do with those cards? How do you follow-up with people? Do you even follow-up with your contacts? Don't think that sending an email the next day is considered follow-up, because if you just stop there, nothing will happen. Don't expect people to pick up the phone and call you just because you spoke for 5 minutes at the event and that you have a great product, because you will be very disappointed.

If you find that you forget to follow-up, your 'fears' probably fall into one of these categories:

- Fear of rejection.
- Lack of confidence in themselves and or their products.
- Fear of competition.
- Expect people to call if they are interested.
- Don't know what to say.
- Don't know when to follow-up and how often.
- Don't even know what a follow-up system is.

Maybe you relate to one or more of those categories, and the reason why you never follow-up with your contacts and permanently struggle to get new clients is hidden in those fears.

Think about this: Imagine you hiring a salesperson to sell your products. She attends 4 events a week, gets hundreds of business cards a week, you think "Great, she'll get lots of clients in no time!"

Then your salesperson comes back to the office, sits at her desk and waits, waits, waits, and waits. After a while you may ask "What are you waiting for?" and she answers "Well I met lots of people last week, so now I wait for them to call, to close the deal, and make a sale."

Would you pay this person to spend hours at the office waiting for the phone to ring? I don't think so! You'll ask her to do her job as a salesperson and go after clients.

You are the salesperson for your own business.

If you don't follow-up, and don't take action to communicate with people to close the deal, you are doing the exact same thing. It's like you are wasting money sitting at your desk.

Again, making contact with new people at networking events is just the first step. It is what you do to follow-up that will lead to make a sale, get more clients and success for your business.

Having an effective follow-up system in place will help you grow your business without wondering what is the next step to connect with people.

CHAPTER 13
3 Easy Ways To Boost Your Networking

Everybody is in agreement that in business, networking plays a determinant factor in your growth and your success. So why do so many people jump from one networking event to another and complain that networking is not working? Networking is a way of life. It is one of the fastest ways to grow your business and one of the most cost-efficient marketing tools.

Here are 3 easy and low cost ways to boost your business with networking:

1. Follow-up

People like big events. They feel great when they enter a room packed with people. Big events are great if your goal is to get a bunch of business cards, but not if you are trying to get business. What do you do with all those cards?

Be honest, most people put them on their desk or in a shoe box, eventually enter the information in their rolodex, but don't do anything with them. Why? Because they collected so many that they are overwhelmed and don't know how or where to start. They just don't have a follow-up system.

Statistics show that we need to hear or see a message at least 7 times in order to notice it. So if you only follow-up 2 or 3 times you're losing business. A networking event is a way of introducing yourself and starting a relationship with the people you meet. You may get a client after an event but usually networking takes time, patience and consistency.

That is why it is important not only to have a follow-up system but also to have a 10 to 16 step follow-up system in place. Some ideas are:

- Send an email in the next 24 hours.
- Send a thank you note (in this age of technology, sending a handwritten thank you note will make you stand out from the crowd).
- Send a postcard
- Send articles or information related to their industry
- Send a newsletter
- Offer free ebooks, videos, or webinars
- And of course, call them!

Be creative in order to follow-up and differentiate yourself from others, especially from your competitors. Stand out from the average entrepreneurs. Be unique!

2. Join a networking group

Personally, I prefer small events because I get more business out of them. That's why I would organize networking events limited to 25 people. Small groups allow you to start a relationship right away, have the time to really introduce yourself and your business, which is more efficient than speaking with somebody for 3 seconds, giving your card to them and then going on to the next person.

Once, I attended an event, where there were about 80 people. I thought I was actually joining a more intimate group, but it was too late to leave. So I decided that my goal would be to speak with 5 people so that way I would have the time for a real conversation. While I was speaking with somebody, a woman came up to me, interrupted our conversation and said, "I just wanted you to have my card." She put her card in my hand and left. She didn't introduce herself, tell me her name, or find out who I was or what I did.

Apparently her goal was to give out as many business cards as she could during the event.

Not only is this very rude, but it's also totally useless. However, I thought maybe she was new to networking and didn't know how it works so I gave her the benefit of the doubt. The next day, I sent her an email to follow-up and to get a chance to learn more about her business. Guess what! She never returned my email and of course never called. So what is the purpose?

No wonder so many people say that networking is not working!

To achieve better results in networking, join a minimum of two groups and commit to them instead of trying to go to every event and meet people only once. Being committed to a group will help you to build a relationship, learn about people, trust them and then do business with them. When you get to know and trust them you will either work with them directly if you need their products or services, or you will give them referrals because you know that if you send people to them they will be satisfied with the result.

3. Create strategic alliances

Would you rather meet a thousand people, one at a time, or meet a few people who each introduce you to a thousand?

Now think about this: What about looking for people who have the same target market as you, but are not your competitors, and offer great complementary products or services to you?

Working with them will be a great opportunity to access their clients or mailing list. You can cross-promote each other, you can organize events together, you can do a mailing campaign together, it is a win/win situation.

Let's say you partner with two new entrepreneurs a month and have access to their client list. (I'm not saying they will sell you their list of clients or prospects, but *through* them you can get exposure to their clients or prospects!) If they have one thousand, two thousand, or even twenty thousand people on their mailing list, instantly, you have access to thousands of people.

When I mention a business in my newsletter, "Biba Recommends", the business I'm promoting gets exposure to thousands of people on my list. People pay more attention because I'm the one who recommended the product or service. The people on my list know me and trust me, so they'll be more likely to learn more about this product or service.

And at the same time, the business I am promoting is promoting my products and services on their newsletter and I get exposure too, to thousands of people that I don't even know!

Instead of looking for one prospect or one client at a time, look for people or businesses you can partner with. Make a list of the businesses that are complementary to yours to create strategic alliances with. Strategic alliances are one of the fastest ways to grow your business.

When you use networking that way, then you don't need to meet everybody in the room. The only thing you need is to find a couple of potential strategic alliances. Look for quality instead of quantity.

CHAPTER 14
Networking From The Road

Networking is more than just putting your business name out there for people to find you. It's also a part of getting to know people who are going to spread the word about what you do, what you sell, and that are going to support you in all that you do. Networking is going to involve getting to know as many people in life as you can, and putting your business in front of those people, so they will represent your name, your business, and will tell others about what you have to offer.

If your business requires that you travel often, or perhaps you travel often to find supplies, visit relatives, or just because you like it you should make it a point to get to know those who you are sitting around you on the plane. Or even those who are sitting on the bench while waiting in the airport.

How are you going to get started on this?

Start the conversation by saying hello, how are you today?

Ask questions. The best way to get to know someone is to ask questions. Without asking questions, it can be difficult to carry on a conversation. Asking questions is a good icebreaker, in turn, the person is going to want to talk about him or herself, and where he or she is traveling. You can then lead into something like, "Is this a business trip or a personal trip?"

As you go on with the conversation, the person is going to ask you questions, which is where you will be able to talk about your business and what you do.

Make it a point to meet at least one new person every day.

You'll to increase your network, which means you'll increase the people you know in life. Increasing your business network is going to be dependent on your abilities to carry on a conversation and to talk with others. Force yourself to do this, if you have to.

Force yourself to stick to your habit of meeting at least one new person a day. As you make this a point, you will make this a habit and in the long run, your business will thrive for it!

CHAPTER 15
Strategies to Maximize Your Social Networking Results

After networking, social media is one of the fastest growing and most inexpensive ways to reach your target market. You can invite people to visit your website, send them a private message, or mention that you already have friends in common. Facebook is the #1 social media website used by millions of people every day.

It's important that you complete you profile with as much information as possible about your business, so when people come to your page, they will see immediately the benefit of being connecting with you.

Social media is pretty much the same as going to a live networking event, and talking to the people you know, and the people they know or introduce you to. However, there are many advantages to e-networking versus live networking.

Compared to a live event, you can view a person's profile before you connect, so it's much easier to contact people in your field, share similar interests, or are in your target market.

Social media can be time consuming at first. But when you know how to use it effectively, it's just a question of 15 minutes a day to follow up with people, send them messages, contact new people, expand your business, promote events, and invite people to seminars, teleclasses, webinars or programs.

It only takes a few hours a week to help your business grow.

Social media has changed the way we interact. People are more willing to work with others they can see from a distance or have friends in common with. It comes down to having common interests or goals while also having a set purpose.

Social media definitely changed the way I network. Since I moved to Miami few years ago, I don't attend as many live networking events. Through social media, I can instantaneously reach a large number of people all over the world.

Another advantage of online networking is that you won't forget names and faces! You have them right in front of you along with what the person does, what they like and dislike, and what their goals are. You don't have to worry about losing someone's business card or forgetting what another person does.

Another advantage of social media is that it costs a lot less than other types of advertising. Every business owner knows that they need to advertise to promote their business but very often the expenses are misdirected because the advertising is not always targeted to the right people.

Social media costs you the time to do research, promotion, and follow-up, so make sure to organize your time wisely in order to be effective without burning yourself out and spending overtime doing it.

The most efficient way to use online social media is to dedicate 15 minutes a day as part of your marketing plan, to promote your business, and stick to it.

PART III
Advanced Networking Techniques

CHAPTER 16
Are You Reflecting The Right Image For Your Business?

I always say, the way we dress is our 1st marketing tool. We have only ONE chance to make the first (right!) impression. So why is it that so many people don't really pay attention to their personal look? Small business owners often pay lot of money to define their business brand, but unfortunately don't think of their personal brand!

Are you one of those people who says that they don't judge a book by its cover? If so, are you really being honest with yourself?

How do you act when you meet someone for the first time? Do you pay attention to his or her general look? I know I do!

Do you know that in life, and more importantly in business, you have only 10 seconds to make the right first impression when you meet someone for the first time? Yes, in just 10 seconds people will subconsciously make a decision on whether they want to work with you or not. So make that first contact count!

How you dress influences what people think about you.

Working with small business owners for years, in France and in the U.S., and specializing in networking and marketing, I have to say that I'm always surprised to see how some people dress for networking events or business meetings. Those who do not dress in suitable business attire are usually the ones who are surprised that their business doesn't take off.

How do you act when you buy a product in a store? Let's say you're looking at a printer and you have the choice between two brands. (The products inside the boxes have the exact same features.) So how do you make your choice?

Do you choose the one with the less attractive package or with the most attractive package? Do you choose the one that highlights the features and benefits of buying this product, or the one that presents the product in a regular white box without any information? It is exactly the same thing where people are concerned.

How a prospect will choose between you and your competitors is not based on your experience and your competencies, but is based on the way you look. If you are able to impress them with the way you dress and the way you look, they will pay more attention to what you have to say. It seems unfair, I know, but remember that you are judged every day, simply on the way you look.

How to maximize your appearance:

1. Create an image to impress!

Your image is what people see long before you even get the chance to speak. Choose a wardrobe that works for you and your business. You need to be yourself. Don't try to copy someone, follow what you see in a magazine, or follow some fashion trends. If your image doesn't reflect your personality, people will see it immediately. Don't try to fake it, be yourself. Create an image that fits your business. Have the right attitude. Be consistent with your image. The image you reflect, good or bad, has a direct impact on how others perceive your business. In other words, have a professional look. Respect yourself and others will respect you.

2. Dress with confidence

When you look your best and act with self-confidence, others will see you that way too. For men or women, having a great suit will give you instant authority. Choose one in a classic style that fits well and suits your body type. Keep it simple. Wear traditional colors like navy (trustworthy), grey (conservative) and black (chic & conservative). If you live in an area like California or Florida where it is sunny all the time, you can use brighter colors, but make sure they're not too flashy and that everything is coordinated.

3. Pay attention to your shoes
Sloppy shoes can completely damage your image. Choose shoes that improve your silhouette. Make sure to clean your shoes before your leave the house.

4. Treat your hands like your best friend.
When you meet someone and hand out your business card, people will have a look at your hands. Have neat, well-polished nails if you are a woman and remember to change your nail polish on a regular basis, if you wear it. Never, ever go out with your nail polish half effaced.

I read once in a magazine that when a man dates a woman for the first time, the first two things he notices are her hands and her shoes! So consider the same thing for business.

You don't need to spend lots of money to look great, business-like, and confident. I work with many start-up businesses and very often my clients tell me that since they have a limited budget for their business, how can they possibly have a budget for a new wardrobe?

Don't buy clothes that will go out of style at the end of the season. Buy a few new tops, ties, or accessories that will make the difference. Sometimes by just changing one item in your outfit, you will look totally different. So you don't need hundreds of clothes; just learn how to put everything together. Think of yourself as a brand.

As a small business owner, you spend a lot of time trying to perfect and improve your offering.

Treat yourself as your most important product.

CHAPTER 17
Networking With Your Previous Clients

Your previous customers are valuable to your future business. As you get each new client, you want to network with that client again in the future, to keep your business in their mind, and to keep them on as a walking and talking billboard for your business.

The future of your business is going to evolve to include repeat clients and referral customers, both of which are vital to the ongoing relationship of your business, the consumer, and the local surroundings of your business.

How can you network with your previous clients?

Even if your clients are online, you can network with your customers. A simple note or email is going to do the trick. Ask about their day, talk with them by name, and offer advice or to continue with the conversation when they have time to chat with you. Talk with your clients about what they have purchased, or what work you have done for them.

Ask if there is anything that can be done to improve the process they went through while dealing with your business.

Network with your largest clients by taking them to lunch, or ordering them something special and having it delivered to their office or home. As you continue to acknowledge your largest clients, they'll keep you fresh in their minds. They'll tell others about what you sent to them and how they feel about your business.

Never forget about your previous clients.

Of course, this is not done with every type of business, but with the largest buyers who are spending thousands of dollars with you.

Keeping the lines of communication open with a previous client is going to increase awareness of your products, and what you have for sale. This in turn is going to increase sales, one repeat client at a time.

In the offline business, and in online business you can network with your previous clients by creating mailing lists and using these mailing lists. State something along the lines of, "Because we have done business in the past, I find that now is the time to offer you this great advantage in Networking we have, and would like to give you a special price!"

Yes this is still advertising, but networking at the same time because you have established a relationship with the customer.

CHAPTER 18
Attending Live Events To Boost Your Business

Do you attend live events to boost your business? If so, you should attend these events to attract more clients, meet new partners and make more money.

Live events can skyrocket your business and change the course of your life forever. By getting to know new people and interacting on the spot, in person, you can showcase your experience and leave people asking about you and your business.

I love Internet and social media, connecting with people via Facebook, Twitter, or LinkedIn. I also know that taking my business to the next level is going to require stepping out of cyberspace and into the realm of live connections.

This is why I focus on live events related to my field of expertise and my target audience at least 2 to 3 times a year. It helps two-fold by first allowing me to learn new strategies from like-minded entrepreneurs and second by providing a great networking opportunity with 200 to 300+ people that I probably wouldn't meet otherwise.

There are many benefits of attending live events across the country. You can refocus your business with tools and tips you learn. Meeting other successful entrepreneurs is guaranteed to give you new perspectives, ideas and strategies to implement in your business model. The goal is to meet people with similar wants for their business and learn from each other. It will be refreshing to swap stories of success and of what doesn't work.

Attending live events is great for any business.

Take live events as an opportunity to widen your list, gain potential clients and start joint ventures. You will find other business owners who have products that compliment yours – don't miss your opportunity to sign up with them, it is a win/win situation. You may also gain a few new friends along the way.

National events are your chance to take your business to the next level. Local networking events are great but don't give you country wide exposure. These events come on a regular basis, so take the chance to meet people from all over the country, and even the world, to promote yourself as the expert outside of your own backyard.

CHAPTER 19
Is Finding A Networking
Group Worth Your Time?

Have you ever considered participating within a networking group? I'm talking about one that is comprised mainly of local professional men and women with the sole purpose of exchanging business ideas and gaining contacts? If not, consider the advantages since it is a low cost and effective way to grow your business.

Let me tell you, I've had some great experiences while networking in this way. Generally, such groups are comprised of about 30 or so members, each from a different profession, sharing practical advice and lessons learned as they establish trust with one another. What a terrific opportunity for a first hand referral as you sharpen your own saw while establishing valuable long term trust-worthy connections. Just think about the last time you needed something repaired in your home and the only source you had was either Yellow Pages or the Internet?

It's easy to be left out in the cold when you consider those options. Just imagine having your own 'database' within a network of trusted professionals who can steer you in the right direction. Think too, about those same professionals talking to their contacts about you!

This is the power of networking within the 'right' group and why an effective networking group will prove to be a valuable resource that keeps on giving. There are some real clues to consider in your quest for finding the perfect networking group.

Maximize the Benefits of a Networking Event

It's about consistency. The best is to belong to two or three groups, attend their events regularly, get to know the other members, and in exchange, they will get to know you and trust you. When you see the same people over and over, you develop a strong relationship with them. The benefit of building relationships with a committed group of people will result in new leads for your business.

It's about patience. The benefit will not appear overnight, and this is why you need to follow up with your contacts. Networking is like dating, one meeting is not enough to know someone. It will probably take some time, some meetings, some lunches or some drinks before you really start doing business together.

Here are some tips on how to maximize the benefits of a networking event:

- Know your goals. Are you looking for leads, partners, new clients, services?
- Bring your business cards and a pen to take notes on the back of the cards you receive.
- Have an effective 15 to 30 second elevator pitch. Learn how to sell yourself before your services or products. People want to hear about you first, and when they know you and trust you, they will buy your services or refer you to someone else.
- Have a web site. Some people will probably want to hear more about your business later, so give them the opportunity to get the information they are looking for.
- Meet people, and ask about their business or services. Be curious and ask about them. People love to speak about themselves, so ask questions and listen to their answers.
- Be a problem solver. People will be more interested in you if you tell them how you can solve their problems instead of just hearing your story.
- Go to people. Don't wait for them to come to you. Some people are very shy. They will be very happy if you make the first move.
- Go to events with a friend, a colleague, a client, and introduce people to each other.

- Send a thank you note or email to your new contacts. Thank them for their time and reintroduce yourself in a few lines. They met lots of people during the event and your business card doesn't say everything about you. So it is good to reinforce your introduction.
- Give them the link to your web site. Tell them about your newsletter, if you have one. This is the best way to stay in touch on a regular basis.
- Schedule follow-up meetings with the people you had a good connection with, or if you think that you can help each other.
- Do it again and again. You will see that networking can expand your contacts, which will definitely help grow your business.
- Be prepared when you attend a networking event.

CHAPTER 20
Are You Wasting Your Time Networking?

Recently, I did a seminar on networking strategies as a guest speaker for an organization. I mentioned that since I moved to Miami, I don't really go to networking events, and even avoid one-on-one meeting.

An attendee asked me: "But how can you tell us to do lot of networking if you don't do it yourself?"

There are lots of ways to network and you don't always need to meet people face to face to do business with them!

These last few years in Miami, I have been working remotely with clients in the US, France, Belgium, Switzerland, Canada and African countries. My clients were finding me via Internet and social media because I promote my business online via articles, blogging, teleclasses, webinars interviews, and more.

I've lived in Miami for 4 years and pretty much didn't know anyone, and as a result I isolated myself. Once I realized this, I joined a couple of networking groups to meet 'real' people.

One thing really surprised me. Most of the people I met said, "Let's meet for a coffee in the next few days so I can tell you more about my business." When I asked if we could do it over the phone, they insisted it had to be in person.

This reminded me of way back, when I started my business in New York, before I knew anything about networking. For the first 6 months I accepted every invitation to coffee. Half a year later, I had nothing to show except a lot of time and money spent at Starbucks!

No clients came out of the effort.

I'm surprised to see people still do the "let's have coffee" technique. When I asked how many clients these networkers got out of coffee meetings most replied "not many" but they explained that it was a good way to meet people.

What's the point of networking?
I thought it was to get clients!

Years ago, when I was still in New York, I learned how to do all of my meetings over the phone, and pre-qualify people before having face-to-face meetings. It's easy to do. I exchange emails and phone calls to see if there is a real reason to meet in person. I accept a meeting only if I know that they're either ready to become clients, we're planning a partnership together, or we have referrals for each other. Anything other than those three reasons can be done over the phone the exact same way without wasting time.

Think about your time. If you go to meet someone and it takes 30-45 minutes to travel there. A 30-minute scheduled meeting normally ends up taking about an hour because you'll start the conversation with small talk, you may be interrupted by people, phones or general noise, and you'll need to order your coffee or tea. Then you'll return to your office or home in 30-45 minutes. By the end of this coffee meet and greet, you've spent 2-3 hours on just one person who 95% of the time won't be converted into a client!

What is your hourly pay? If you normally make $150 hour, you've just spent $450 on a cup of coffee!

What can you say in person that you can't say over the phone or on Skype?

One person at this event said he had to meet with me in person to show me the documents. Why not do that over the Internet and save time and money? During a call, you can send documents in PDF or PowerPoint format. If you have the feeling you really need to see the person while you talk to her, use Skype.

I asked him if he was offering his services in other states, because I could have some referrals from him, but not locally. He said "Yes of course I can offer my services to anybody, anywhere", but at the same time telling me that he couldn't explain it over the phone, we had to meet. How can he offer services to people out of state? It doesn't make sense to me.

I've never met 98% of my clients face-to-face, but I've been working with most of them for years. I help clients from France, Belgium, or Switzerland start businesses all over the U.S. by walking them through my systems. We work over the phone or Skype, and transfer all documents via the Internet.

A woman I met on Facebook, only meets people over the phone for 15 to 30 minutes for what she calls "virtual coffee" meeting. She has 5 to 10 "virtual coffees" a week and not only grows her business this way, but has created a program to teach this strategy to her clients. After we met on Facebook, we had a couple of virtual coffees together (we both actually live in Miami) but we've never met in person. We worked on a few projects together and were able to build those projects without face-to-face meeting.

Find out if meeting face-to-face is working for you!

Check your calendar and calculate how many hours a week you spend meeting people face-to-face. Then tally up how many of them become paying clients or send you referrals.

Then, for one month do your best to schedule as many, if not all, of those meetings over the phone instead. By the end of the month you should be able to see how much time you gained that will allow you to get productive tasks done, such as writing articles, promoting your business, working on your marketing plan, creating new services or products, and working with your current clients that are paying you.

Most solo-entrepreneurs always say that they don't have enough time in a day to do what they have to do. My motto is work differently and you will have all the time you need!

CHAPTER 21
A Lead Generation System That Works

I recently had a drink with somebody that I had met four years ago, when I started my business in New York, but whom I didn't get the opportunity to see for a couple of years. He was one of the first subscribers to my newsletter, so even if we hadn't seen each other for a while, he was reading the newsletter every week and stayed informed of what was happening in my business.

One of his comments was "Wow, I can't believe how much you have grown your business! I remember when you started, just moving from France, and you didn't know anybody here. How did you get to this point? You definitely can't do all of this on your own, so how many people work for you now? What is your secret?"

I answered that I found my result a normal growth. You work hard, you learn from others, you implement the techniques and strategies that you have learned, and if you do it correctly, the normal result is to grow.

But when I got back home, I thought about it. What did I do for the past couple of years to grow my business, to the point that I actually made the same revenue in the last three months as I had made all last year? I must have done something!

And it comes down to my lead generation system:

1. I exchange links with other entrepreneurs in my target market.

These businesses have the same target market, but are not my competitors. So when people visit their websites, they see my link and come to check my website.

2. I have an opt-in box on each page of my website.

And since I never know when a visitor will decide to sign-up for the newsletter, I make sure that I don't miss any opportunity!

3. I offer a free ebook and videos.

To make sure people actually sign up, I offer them something that interests them, inform them, and help them solve one of their problems.

My ebook "15 Ways to Instantly Skyrocket Your Networking Results" (www.bibapedron.com/free-gift) is free for them, but at the same time shows them what I do, how I can help them, and how to get more clients with networking.

4. I send a weekly newsletter.

People sign up first to get the free ebook. After that, it is my job to tell them more about my business, and share resources, marketing and networking information in order to build a relationship with them. Statistics show that when people don't buy immediately, they will buy in the next 12 months. So I need to make sure that I am always in the top of their mind, so when they are ready to buy, they will buy from me.

5. I use auto-responders to automate my website.

I use auto-responders when people sign-up for the newsletter. I set up a series of information messages about my products or services and the benefit of using them. I use them to send audio postcards, to offer special reports for free, and/or to thank my clients for their purchases. Any message will remind them about my services and, more importantly, remind them to come back and buy again. This series of follow-up messages reinforces my relationship with my clients.

6. I send "Thank You" notes to my clients after they buy from me.

In this age of technology, sending a handwritten "Thank You" note makes you stand out from the crowd. You want to impress your clients or contacts and want them to remember you.

7. I ask my clients for testimonials.

Testimonials from satisfied clients are typically the best way to promote your business, and it doesn't cost you a thing. Stop selling and let your clients do it for you.

8. I write articles and post them on directories of articles.

Writing articles is actually one of the best ways that I found to get free exposure. Each article is a way to share my expertise with people, and again, to give a sample of what I do and how I can help them.

9. I publish a press release on various websites.

I do this each time I have a new product. As with the articles, it is a way to get free exposure and inform people, and the press, of what is new in my business.

10. I do public speaking.

This is not my favorite, so I try not to speak four times a month. I schedule a public engagement every other month, so another organization will promote me in their newsletter.

12. I offer a free 30-minute strategy session.

People don't buy from people they don't know, so offering a free strategy session breaks the fear. They can share their goals and challenges with me. I inform them of all the steps. They see how I can help them, and in doing so, I start building a relationship. As a result, 40% become clients after these sessions.
www.bibapedron.com/free-strategy-session

13. I have an Affiliate Program so other people can sell my programs.

Having an Affiliate Program is the easiest and fastest way to increase sales and increase your profits. Your affiliates promote your products or services for free and you don't pay them until they generate a sale for you. When they make a sale, you will be more than happy to pay them a commission, since you would probably never have had this client otherwise.

14. I have a 10-step follow-up system that works.

Statistics show that we need to hear or see a message 10 to 16 times in order to notice it. If you only follow-up two or three times, you're losing opportunities to turn prospects into clients. That is why it is important not only to have a follow-up system, but to have at least a 10-step follow-up system in place.

What is YOUR lead generation system?

Take some times to sit and think about it. Are you using 2 or 3 lead generation techniques, or do you have 10 to 15? Which of your lead generation techniques works the best for your business? What other techniques could you implement?

Schedule a new technique each month, set up a date to make sure you will respect your marketing calendar, track the result for each technique, see what works for your business, and watch your sales grow!

CHAPTER 22
How To Measure Your Networking Effectiveness

Performance metrics are those measurements that will tell you whether your efforts are resulting in business. Networking and relationship marketing are time-intensive so you want to spend that time wisely. Performance metrics are the keys to this analysis.

Your networking should include a variety of business organizations. To find out which ones of these are worth pursuing you need to define, measure, and evaluate key performance metrics. These performance metrics need to be measured on a regular basis. Marketing through organizations and through networking is a marketing medium just like direct mail, e-mail, offline, or print media.

Your marketing plan would certainly include analyzing performance metrics for your advertising through television, radio, newspapers, and magazines. Similar performance metrics for networking must also be monitored.

Example Performance Metrics
- Direct costs associated with the networking
- Number of events attended
- Number of contacts generated

- Number of sales leads generated
- Number of referrals
- Number of sales
- Number of service contracts
- Dollars generated from direct contacts
- Dollars generated from referrals

Analyze your performance metrics per organization on a regular basis. Six months is a decent time horizon. If the performance metrics don't show promise within this time frame, drop that particular organization and move on.

Stop spending so much time with organizations that aren't working out. Foster deeper ties with those organizations and events that show the highest returns. Your performance metrics will separate the duds from the performers very quickly.

By tracking performance metrics you can determine very easily which of your networking efforts are paying off and which are simply eating up your time and energy.

CHAPTER 23
Reactivate Your Network During The Holidays

If you haven't reached your networking goals by November you can reactivate your skills during the holiday season.

I guess that like most entrepreneurs, at the beginning of the year, you wrote a long list of goals for the year; new things you would be excited to do, new strategies you planned to implement to get plenty of new clients and grow your business.

It is time for you to take stock. Are you on track with your goals? Are you half way there or did you get caught in your routine and forgot all about those goals? Did your goals change since you last evaluated?

It is not too late!

Don't be overwhelmed by the holiday season. Yes, most people who do not have businesses centered on holiday goods and services slow down for the holiday season, but it is the perfect time to give a last boost to finish out the year on a high note.

Take your list back out, check it twice... No really, check each goal and rate it from 1 to 10 to see how far you are from achievement (1 being not started and 10 being complete). Select the 3 that rate the most and concentrate on those only. What could you do to reach those goals by the end of December? Whatever your goals (whether they be to get more clients, create new products, start a marketing plan, etc.) they are all related to your network. You can have the best product in the world, but if you don't have clients you have no business. You get clients simply by building your list and your network which is filled with people who like you, trust you and will work with you or refer clients to you.

How did you focus your networking this year?

How many events did you attend, how many business cards did you collect, how many follow-up meetings did you schedule, and how many new clients did you get from your networking efforts. It is time to look back on what happened since the beginning of the year. Take this opportunity to organize and update your database. Make sure to take all the business cards you collected off your shelves or shoe boxes and create a database to set up a concrete follow-up system.

How can you reactivate all of your contacts and implement your follow-up system?

Send a greeting card just to say "Hi."

Important: don't try to sell anything. You are here to build a relationship, not to do a sale pitch. Ask them how you could help. It is ALL ABOUT THEM, NOT YOU. A couple of weeks after the card, give them a call to learn more about their business. Listen to what they say and take notes to find out what you can do for them. Then write your notes down to use them later in your follow-up system.

If you know that their birthday is coming up, send them a birthday card. People always like attention. The recipient will be impressed, and you will be number one on their list when they will need your service or will have a referral for you.

Send a Holiday card, if it is the one action you will take by the end of the year, don't miss this opportunity. Even if you didn't see them or speak with them for months, it is the perfect time to reactivate the connection and come back to the top of their mind. Don't forget to put them on your follow-up system so by next year you won't be months without keeping in touch with them on a regular basis.

Use the last two months to effectively implement your follow-up system, if you don't have one yet, so you will be ready to start the next year as a successful networker. This strategy will give you more time to work on your marketing plan or to promote your product or service and grow your business.

The advantage of having a follow-up system in place, is that you work on it once, then your system is doing the work for you, telling you what to do with all of your contacts and when to do it. That will free up a lot of your time.

PART IV
Next Steps & Moving Forward

CHAPTER 24
In Review: How to Skyrocket Your Networking Effort

1. The #1 success of networking is to show up.

When you join a group or an organization it's important you commit to the group and attend the meetings on a regular basis.

In order to build relationships with other members, they need to meet you more than once and you need to meet them more than once. The more times you attend the meetings, the more you'll get results. At each meeting, you'll learn a little more about them and their business and they'll learn more about you. The more they see you, the more they know about you, the more they trust you, the more referrals they'll give you.

2. Always arrive prepared.

Conduct some research before you decide to attend an event; you'll want to know ahead of time what kind of people will be attending. Are they in your target market, will you face a lot of competitors, or do you have a clear way to stand out from the crowd?

Spend some time on the website of the event's organizing group learn about them. Do they specialize in a specific industry? Does the group focus on small and intimate events or do they pack the room with hundreds of people?

Sometimes I have people who come to my events and are surprised to see only 12 to 15 people. It's right there on my website that the small setting is what makes Biba4Network and our meetings different from other groups' meetings. On our home page we mention: "Because networking is more than just shaking hands and collecting business cards, most of our events are limited to 15 people, to drive better results. There's more time to introduce yourself and your business to the group, more time to get to know each other, so more time to get business." If they had looked at the website first, they would have known our style and wouldn't have been surprised or disappointed.

When you go to an event, it is also important to have one or two goals in mind. Are you looking for leads, partners, new clients, services? You won't approach people the same way depending on your goal. You want to be sure to send the right message and use your time wisely.

3. Never leave home without your business cards.

I've said it before: it doesn't matter where you're going, ALWAYS have your cards with you! You never know where you'll meet an interesting new contact and you don't want to miss the opportunity to exchange cards.

Carry a pen to take notes on the back of the cards you receive; something you want to remember about the person, something they said, and something you promised to send them.

4. Have an effective elevator pitch.

We talked about this earlier in the book and this is one of the keys to successful networking. Remember to introduce yourself, and tell them the old adage "What's in it for me" or more accurately, "what's in it for them." People want to learn about you: what you're about, what you can do before they make a purchase or consider referring you to one of their valuable contacts.

When you tell others about your business, be passionate, energized and energetic. Personalize your story so that your new contacts can picture themselves as part of your story. This will help them become a part of your mission.

Then once they know you and trust you, they will either buy your services or if they don't need what you offer; they will (hopefully) refer someone else to you. If they trust you, this trust will appear in the message they send to others.

Don't have only one elevator pitch but 3 or 4, to be able to adapt your message depending of your audience.

5. DO NOT SELL.

I said it before, but I will repeat it again: DO NOT SELL. Networking events are not places to sell. Do not give a sales pitch. Just introduce yourself, who you are, what you do, how you can help people. You attend these meetings and gatherings to get contacts and build relationships, not to sell.

6. Meet people, make connections, ask about their business or services. Be curious, ask about them.

People love to talk about themselves so ask questions and more importantly, listen to their answers. Use those answers to see how you can help them, how you can assist them, what resources you can share with them. As I mentioned earlier, this will always come back to help you. People you meet will be able to help you, give you referrals and resources, even if is it not today, the time will come.

7. Be a problem solver.

People are more interested in you if you tell them how you can solve their problems and challenges instead of just telling them your story. Stand out from the crowd. In the long run, you'll win all the business you desire.

8. Go to people; don't wait for them to come to you.

Some people are very shy and they'll be happy if you make the first move. Remember people attend networking meetings to meet other people and expand their circle of contacts. Help them make it easier for others to meet you.

9. Go to events with a friend, colleague, or client and introduce people to each other.

You will be considered a "Pro Networker." People will think you know almost everybody and as a result other people will come to speak with you. This tactic puts you in the center of the group and brings people to you.

10. Present a professional image.

Maintain a brochure and/or website. Some people will probably want to learn more about your business later, so give them the opportunity to get the information in a format they can digest on their own timetable. Make it easy for people to get to know you.

I become frustrated when I meet someone and can't understand what they do. Sometimes the reason is because we met only for a few seconds or because I just didn't understand. Remember English is not my first language, so sometimes I can get "lost in translation."

But other times I don't understand because they weren't clear when they described their business. When I return home and want to look at their website to learn more about them, I notice that they don't have a website. If you don't have a website now, put this high on your to-do list. In the meantime, at least create a brochure.

11. Project the right image, make the right impression, and create the right impact.

What makes you unique? Every person I have ever met is different from all the other people I know. Everyone is unique in one way or another. This carries over into the business you create. When you display your individualism, your best traits, you'll stand out from the crowd. When you are proactive, you'll meet many new people, and you'll ensure they remember you.

12. In the 24 to 48 hours after an event send a 'thank you' note or email to your new contacts.

Thank them for their time and reintroduce yourself in a few lines. They probably met many people during the event and your business card cannot say everything about you, especially if you had a meaningful conversation with the person. So, it's worthwhile to reinforce your introduction and reestablish that connection.

Give them the link to your website so they can learn more about you and your business. Tell them about your newsletter and invite them to subscribe. That will be the best way to stay in touch on a regular basis, so they will always know what you are up to. Hopefully, they'll forward your publication to others and expand your network further.

13. Follow-up, follow-up, follow-up.

Schedule follow-up meetings with people you had a good connection with or if you think you can help each other. Put an organizational and a follow-up system in place; don't become overwhelmed with all your business cards.

Develop your A, B, C lists to know how often you should contact people and reconnect with them. Follow up as soon as possible when someone gives you a referral. Your contact took the time to give you a referral, so don't spoil it; contact the referral source to thank them and then let them know how your interaction went. If the association works well, they'll be glad to be part of the success and more than happy to give you more contacts in the future. Volunteer to give them contacts in return.

14. Look at the big picture - Create partnerships.

Instead of looking for a potential client and working with people one at a time, look for other professionals with whom you can create partnerships.

Look for others to cross-promote your business: entrepreneurs who have businesses that complement yours, but who are not competitors or someone who has the same or similar target market as you. If you cross-promote each other, instead of having access to one potential prospect at a time, you'll have access to their entire mailing list, 100's or 1,000's of people, who are your exact target market.

Organize events together: seminars, workshops, and teleclasses. You'll get more exposure in less time.

15. Do it again and again.

You'll see how networking will expand your contacts and will help you grow your business.

CHAPTER 25
It's Time To Get Started!

Congratulations, you made it to the end of the book! You're ready to go out there and not just network, but network effectively! If you are driven to become a successful entrepreneur, nothing will stop you. As Zig Ziglar wrote "See you at the top!" Reading this book is a great first step!

To help you take your skills and your business to the next level, as a free bonus, I want to offer you a series of 3 interviews to learn more how to use networking and social media effectively. Including one interview with Ivan Misner, founder of BNI and one interview with Bog Burg author of Endless referrals. Two men who are masters at networking.

Get your free bonus at http://bibapedron.com/book-bonuses

And to help you a step further, I prepared a workbook "Power of Networking Secrets" a 7-step follow up system to turn your contacts into paying clients, including a 30 days unlimited emails follow-up, to answer all of your questions. To make sure that you will not only read this book but also that you implement the strategies you learned and make money.

Get "Power of Networking Secrets" at http://bibapedron.com/pon

Biba's Abbreviated Step-by-Step Networking Playbook:

1. Get comfortable being alone while taking in the sights and sounds of the room for the first 5 minutes;

2. Pick out 2-3 shy looking people in the room that you will network with;

3. Begin your conversations with your prepared or ad-libbed line about a specific characteristic of the person or something/someone interesting within sight;

4. Introduce yourself and let them introduce themselves;

5. Give a brief description of your business, but not too much! You want to keep them interested in learning more;

6. Exchange your contact information and be sure to get their information;

7. On the back of their business card write down three key elements: 1/The date and time you met, 2/ categorize their urgency in your business needs, 3/ jot down something that struck you about the person's business that you will remember them by;

8. Close the conversation and let them go meet other people. Now go talk to someone else before the shyness bug bites you again!

Work With Biba

Since I started my first business in 1998, I have grown two international businesses specializing in helping people like you develop their business with effective networking, social media branding, and marketing strategies. I am recognized in France as one of the top female business coach and marketing expert.

I have shared my business strategies with hundreds of people and guided them to tweaking those strategies to their own businesses. When you discover my systems, you will be excited and amazed at how easily you connect with your target market, expand your business, and double your revenue.

I'm also an international best-selling author!

My goal is to help and advise you on all aspect of your own business to show you the strategies that I use over and over again for myself in my successful 6-figure international businesses and that I teach to my clients. This is your chance to learn how to boost your income, network effectively, attract more clients and get your brand known.

To learn more about how you can work with me to grow your business, please visit me at www.TheConnectionQueen.com

If you want more visibility, more clients, and more money, I'm also offering you a complimentary 30-minute session with me. Just go to http://bibapedron.com/free-strategy-session to sign up!

About The Author

Biba Pédron was born and raised in France. For over 15 years, she has served as a sales & marketing manager for a number of companies in her native France. Recognized as someone who powerfully connects with people, professionally and socially, Biba brings her successful networking techniques to both sides of the Atlantic.

With great passion and drive, and little English language speaking skills, she moved to the U.S. in 2003 and within two years became known as "The Connection Queen" and published her first book, "Start Your Dream Business Today" which became an #1 best seller.

Business coach & marketing expert, Biba helps countless small business owners, entrepreneurs and professionals connect the dots of marketing, social media, networking, and branding to grow their business, teaching simple but effective marketing strategies that really work. So they can attract more clients online and offline while building a 6-figure business. All while following their passion and doing what they love best.

Biba Pédron knows from experience that the majority of businesses don't succeed because they lack the right tools and the right system needed to excel. This is why she offers entrepreneurs, key business secrets needed to build their business and give them the exact formula they need to grow their business in a step-by-step road map, leaving them with no way to get lost or take a wrong turn.

Over the past 10 years she not only taught networking and marketing strategies to her clients, she also connected thousands of entrepreneurs to build international partnerships.

Biba is the author of "Start Your Dream Business Today", "Power of Networking Secrets", "15 Ways to Instantly Skyrocket Your Networking Results", "Top 10 Closet Must-Haves to Successful Business Style", and various books in French.

To learn more about Biba, please visit www.BibaPedron.com

Other Title From Biba

Start Your Dream Business Today!
Must-Know Strategies to Launch a Successful Business
(And Tips To Keep It Running!)
Revised Second Edition

Print Edition: ISBN-13: 978-1500504380
Kindle Edition: ASIN: B00NID27KC

www.ingramcontent.com/pod-product-compliance
Lightning Source LLC
Chambersburg PA
CBHW070835180526
45168CB00002B/845